★★★ Baseball's ★★★
GREATEST TEAMS

★★★ Baseball's ★★★
GREATEST TEAMS

Nate Aaseng

Lerner Publications Company
Minneapolis

Page 1: Before Babe Ruth and Lou Gehrig (4) showed up, no American League batter had ever hit more than 16 home runs in a season. But during their years with the Yankees, these two combined for more than 1,100 home-run trots!
Page 2: Carrying on the Yankee tradition, Mickey Mantle accepts handshakes from Roger Maris and Yogi Berra after adding his 54th home run to the 1961 Yankees' record barrage.

To Mark Lerner

Library of Congress Cataloging-in-Publication Data

Aaseng, Nathan.
  Baseball's greatest teams.

  (Sports talk)
  Summary: Includes profiles of eight teams that the
author considers to be the greatest in the history of
major league baseball.
  1. Baseball—United States—Clubs—History—Juvenile
literature. [1. Baseball—History] I. Title.
II. Series.
GV875.A1A22   1986   796.357′64′0973   84-23326
ISBN 0-8225-1526-1 (lib.bdg.)

Manufactured in the United States of America

1 2 3 4 5 6 7 8 9 10 96 95 94 93 92 91 90 89 88 87 86

★★★ Contents ★★★

"Dare you to do that again!" said baseball experts after Cleveland won an American League
record 111 games in 1954. The Tribe couldn't. Their failure to win another pennant—
plus their horrid 1954 World Series showing—reduced their fine season to an obscure bit of trivia.

Introduction

Competitive sports are really carefully controlled experiments designed to answer one question: Who is the best? Baseball has come up with a 162-game season plus play-offs and a World Series to decide that question. When the year is over, one team is the winner, and there's no way to argue about it.

But those results don't satisfy the baseball fan's interest in finding out who is the *best*. Sure, one team played the best for that one season. But which is the *absolute* top team of all time? Who played the game better than it had ever been played before or since? Unfortunately, it's impossible to compare under the same conditions every team that has ever played. All we can do is guess.

Although there's no way one can be proven wrong in this guesswork, there is still a great risk in naming the top teams of all time. Baseball fans take their game seriously, so a person had better have volumes of facts to back up an opinion, or an irate fan may send him or her sheepishly crawling back to an encyclopedia.

In tackling this treacherous task, I've used four main tests to measure greatness:

1. Has a team clearly stood out from its rivals? To be the best, a team must have won an unusual number of games and piled up awesome statistics. And their lineup must have included some players of Hall of Fame ability.

2. Were they consistent? Philadelphia A's manager Connie Mack was one of the first to insist that the mark of a great team was whether it could repeat a championship season. Each of the eight teams in this book won several pennants in a row. Although the 1954 Cleveland Indians set an American League record of 111 wins, they are not included because they did not win another pennant in the 1950s.

3. Did they win under pressure? Each of these teams came through at least once when it really counted: in a World Series. Although the 1906 Cubs and 1931 A's lost the World Series in the year chosen as their greatest, these same players won the fall classic other years.

4. Did they *earn* their honors? There's no satisfaction in beating weak opponents, no matter how impressive the statistics may seem. The St. Louis Cardinals of the 1940s were edged out of the top eight on this point. World War II took so many good players out of

Led by steady Stan Musial (front row, second from left), the St. Louis Cardinals claimed four pennants and three World Series wins from 1941 to 1946. Not everyone was impressed, however. After all, World War II had drawn away so many top pros that even the usually hapless St. Louis Browns made it to a World Series in 1944. Shown here is the 1942 team.

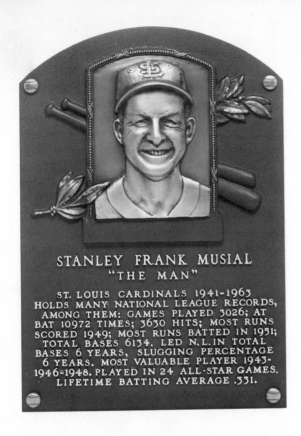

STANLEY FRANK MUSIAL
"THE MAN"

ST. LOUIS CARDINALS 1941-1963
HOLDS MANY NATIONAL LEAGUE RECORDS,
AMONG THEM: GAMES PLAYED 3026; AT
BAT 10972 TIMES; 3630 HITS; MOST RUNS
SCORED 1949; MOST RUNS BATTED IN 1951;
TOTAL BASES 6134. LED N.L.IN TOTAL
BASES 6 YEARS, SLUGGING PERCENTAGE
6 YEARS. MOST VALUABLE PLAYER 1943-
1946=1948. PLAYED IN 24 ALL-STAR GAMES.
LIFETIME BATTING AVERAGE .331.

the league that major league talent was spread thin. In 1945 there weren't even enough stars available to hold an All-Star game! The Yankees' string of titles in the 1950s were at the expense of weak opponents. At their worst on August 2, 1958, the Yankees were the only American League team with a winning record.

Another reason why several great Yankee teams have been left out is because of repetition. Many of the best Yankee squads of the 1930s started as holdovers from the 1927 team, and some 1961 Yankees were playing as early as

1947. In such cases, I have tried to select the best team of an era.

Besides giving highlights of these fine teams, this book explores how great teams are formed. Some will be surprised to learn the role that money has played in building legends. How important has scouting, minor league organization, luck, courage, and foresight been in putting wins in the record book? Who are the poor souls who unwittingly helped these top teams by agreeing to terrible trades?

Considering the number of champions baseball has had, one must be either brave or foolish to try to select the top eight of all time. Carrying the courage or foolishness a step further, this book attempts to stir things up even more by rating these top eight. Read on and see what goes into creating the best teams in baseball.

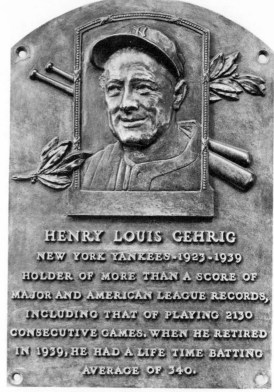

GEORGE HERMAN (BABE) RUTH
BOSTON—NEW YORK, A.L.; BOSTON, N.L.
1915—1935
GREATEST DRAWING CARD IN HISTORY OF
BASEBALL. HOLDER OF MANY HOME RUN
AND OTHER BATTING RECORDS. GATHERED
714 HOME RUNS IN ADDITION TO FIFTEEN
IN WORLD SERIES.

HENRY LOUIS GEHRIG
NEW YORK YANKEES • 1923-1939
HOLDER OF MORE THAN A SCORE OF
MAJOR AND AMERICAN LEAGUE RECORDS,
INCLUDING THAT OF PLAYING 2130
CONSECUTIVE GAMES. WHEN HE RETIRED
IN 1939, HE HAD A LIFE TIME BATTING
AVERAGE OF 340.

The 1927 New York Yankees. Front row (left to right): Julie Wera, Mike Gazella, Pat Collins, Bennett (mascot), Benny Bengough, Ray Morehart, Myles Thomas, Cedric Durst. Middle row: Urban Shocker, Joe Dugan, Earle Combs, Coach O'Leary, Manager Miller Huggins, Coach Fletcher, Mark Koenig, Dutch Ruether, Johnny Grabowski, George Pipgras. Back row: Lou Gehrig, Herb Pennock, Tony Lazzeri, Wilcy Moore, Babe Ruth, Don Miller, Bob Meusel, Bob Shawkey, Waite Hoyt, Joe Giard, Ben Paschal, Styborski, Doc Woods (trainer).

★★★ 1 ★★★

Five O'Clock Lightning

The 1927 New York Yankees

The streaking Chicago White Sox had closed to within one game of the Yankees when they arrived in New York for a June series. Their proud pitching staff looked forward to the challenge of facing New York's "Murderer's Row" lineup. During one of these games, it was the White Sox who pounded the ball as they took an 11-6 lead into the ninth inning. Fans in many ball parks would have filed out in disgust, but Yankee fans merely inched forward in their seats. It was just about time for "Five O'clock Lightning," the Yankees' famous late rally.

Sure enough, Tony Lazzeri cracked his third home run of the game, and New York went on to win, 12-11. This latest attack of Five O'clock Lightning (at that time, all games were played in the afternoon) sent the White Sox spinning out of the pennant race. They simply were no match for the 1927 Yankees, a team considered by most to be the best in baseball history.

Looking back at the strength of Babe Ruth, Lou Gehrig, and friends, it is hard to imagine that the New York club was *not* necessarily the favorite to win the American League pennant that year. Experts looked forward to a close race with at least three teams close to the Yanks in ability. The veteran Washington Senators, Connie Mack's rebuilt Philadelphia A's, and the hard-throwing White Sox each had support as the league's best.

Before we laugh at this prediction, we have to consider how things must have looked in the spring of 1927. The New York attack was built around a carefree superstar who had just turned 32. Since that star had refused to take care of his body, he was expected to continue fading from his peak years in the early 1920s. New York's other outfielders had batted .315 and .299 in 1926, sickly marks compared to the Philadelphia and Washington outfields.

There were three unproven infielders in the Yankee lineup; two had been the goats in the 1926 World Series loss. The fourth infielder was nearing retirement, and none of the catchers belonged in a championship lineup. Yankee pitching was also creaking; two of the top starters were 36 and 33. Their top reliever was almost 30, but as yet he had not pitched in the majors.

What happened to this unpromising roster in 1927 was that everything came together at the same time. Veterans bounced back to enjoy brilliant years while young players burst onto the scene. The result was an awesome group that led a tough league in nearly every category.

This best of all teams could be traced back to, of all things, a series of Broadway plays. A theater fanatic named Harry Frazee bought the Boston Red Sox when they were the champions of baseball. This new owner wasn't as interested in baseball as he was in producing plays,

however. Unfortunately, plays cost a great deal of money, and Frazee found himself piling up debts. To keep his theaters in business, Frazee began to peddle his ball players to the highest bidder.

The highest bidder at the time was Colonel Jacob Ruppert, owner of a very ordinary New York Yankee club. In 1920 Ruppert agreed to pay Frazee $110,000 as well as a $300,000 loan in exchange for a huge, skinny-legged right fielder named Babe Ruth. Fresh from setting a league home-run record of 29 in 1919, Ruth proved to be well worth the price. Within two years, he was the most famous man in the game's history, and he attracted five times the number of fans that the Yanks had been drawing.

Rarely, if ever, has a player soared so far above his rivals. When Babe won the American League title with 54 homers in 1920, tops in the National League was 15! In only his third year as an outfielder, Ruth held baseball's *career* record for home runs. The loud, hilarious Ruth was a legend in more ways than one. A Yankee assigned to stay with him on road trips claimed that he roomed with Ruth's suitcase; the Babe was always out living it up.

The Babe dominated baseball—no matter what position he played. Playing for the Red Sox in 1918, Ruth tied the league lead in home runs and then hurled 29⅔ consecutive shutout innings in the World Series.

Over the next few years, the cash-poor Red Sox also sent pitchers Waite Hoyt and Herb Pennock and third baseman Joe Dugan to the Yanks. Pennock, a smooth, crafty, left-hander, joined the hard-throwing Hoyt as the aces of the New York staff. Both went on to enter baseball's Hall of Fame. Dugan contributed fine fielding at his third-base spot.

The Yankees had a few stars of their own to add to these Red Sox veterans. Since he often was on base when Babe came to bat, speedy center fielder Earle Combs became known as Ruth's table-setter. Left fielder Bob Meusel, a mysterious character who almost never spoke, was deadly at throwing out base runners and was the man who interrupted Ruth's string of homerun titles in 1925.

Then three young infielders all rushed onto the scene at once. The most famous was a shy, awkward first baseman named Lou Gehrig. In his third full year with the Yankees, Gehrig suddenly showed home-run power matched only by Ruth. Second baseman Tony Lazzeri and shortstop Mark Koenig were able to live down their disastrous rookie World Series years and become solid performers in the field and at bat.

In June of 1925, reserve Lou Gehrig filled in for a game while starting first baseman Wally Pipp sat out with a headache. It was 14 years before anyone but Gehrig started a game at first base for the Yankees.

At the same time, New York uncovered a 29-year-old rookie pitcher, Wilcy Moore. At long last, Moore had unexpectedly perfected a sinker ball that made him especially tough in relief.

New York did not have to wait long for a test in 1927. First on the schedule was Philadelphia, loaded with stars such as Lefty Grove, Al Simmons, Ty Cobb, and Mickey Cochrane. The rest of the league should have suspected trouble when the Yankees blasted the A's and won their first 6 games of the year. With that kind of a start, the Yanks held first place through the entire 154-game schedule!

After the White Sox made their brief June challenge, the last hope for a pennant race was Washington. Enjoying a 10-game winning streak, the Senators arrived in New York in midsummer. But it was as if they had walked into a buzz saw. The Yankees ended their charge with wins of 12-1 and 21-1! Washington was so crushed by the defeats that they began drawing lots to choose their batting order. The St. Louis Browns might as well have done the same for all the luck they had against New York, who won 21 straight from St. Louis that season.

Around the horn in the Yankee infield. Left to right: Gehrig (first base), powerful Tony Lazzeri (second base), steady Mark Koenig (shortstop), and defensive ace Joe Dugan (third base).

Despite the lack of a pennant race, the Murderer's Row crew made 1927 a year of unusual thrills. Ruth and Gehrig, the two lefty sluggers, kept hitting home runs at an unbelievable pace. Fans turned out by the thousands as their home-run duel heated up throughout the summer. At 45 to Babe's 44, Gehrig held a late lead, but he finally fell into a slump. Ruth, meanwhile, kept building up steam. He finally broke his own record of 59 with his 60th home run, a record that was to stand for over 30 years.

To get an idea of how the Five O'clock Lightning attack wiped out opponents,

Ruth hit more home runs than any other *team* in the league. Gehrig finished second in the home-run race with 47, and Yankee Lazzeri took third with 18! Led by Gehrig's .373, Ruth's .356, Combs' .356, Meusel's .337, and Lazzeri's .309, New York batted .307 as a team. Gehrig also topped the League with 175 runs batted in.

Although the 1927 Yankees are remembered for their power, New York's pitching also outclassed league foes. They easily led the league in earned run average with Hoyt (2.63) and Urban Shocker (2.84) finishing first and second.

WAITE CHARLES HOYT
"SCHOOLBOY"

NEW YORK YANKEE PITCHER 1921-1930.
LIFETIME RECORD: 237 GAMES WON, 182
GAMES LOST, .566 AVERAGE, EARNED RUN
AVERAGE 3.59. PITCHED 3 GAMES IN 1921
WORLD SERIES AND GAVE NO EARNED RUNS.
ALSO PITCHED FOR BOSTON, DETROIT AND
PHILADELPHIA A.L. AND BROOKLYN,
NEW YORK AND PITTSBURGH N.L.

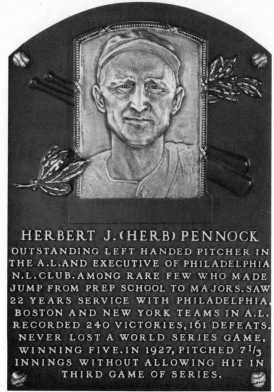

HERBERT J. (HERB) PENNOCK
OUTSTANDING LEFT HANDED PITCHER IN
THE A.L. AND EXECUTIVE OF PHILADELPHIA
N.L. CLUB. AMONG RARE FEW WHO MADE
JUMP FROM PREP SCHOOL TO MAJORS. SAW
22 YEARS SERVICE WITH PHILADELPHIA,
BOSTON AND NEW YORK TEAMS IN A.L.
RECORDED 240 VICTORIES, 161 DEFEATS.
NEVER LOST A WORLD SERIES GAME,
WINNING FIVE. IN 1927, PITCHED $7\frac{1}{3}$
INNINGS WITHOUT ALLOWING HIT IN
THIRD GAME OF SERIES.

Hoyt posted a record of 22-7, spitballer Shocker was 18-6, Moore, 19-7, and Pennock, 19-8, giving New York the top *four* in winning percentage.

Such numbers were too much for the National League to believe. They hooted it was only the weakness of the American League that made the Yankees look good. How else could a team win 110 and lose 44 and finish 19 games ahead of the pack?

But in the World Series, the Pittsburgh Pirates found out the Yankees were for real. Led by two home runs from Ruth and seven innings of no-hit ball by

Pennock, the Yankees became the first American League team to win a series in four straight games.

While the Yankees were rolling to another easy pennant in 1928, some people were suggesting the team be broken up for the good of the game. Even the National League began to agree when New York swept a second-straight series in 1928, this time against St. Louis. Since then, few have been willing to argue that the great New York team of Ruth, Gehrig, Hoyt, Pennock, and the rest of the Five O'clock Lightning was not the best of all time.

THE 1927 NEW YORK YANKEES

Dynasty Years: 1926-1928

World Series Record:
1926 lost to St. Louis Cardinals, 4 games to 3
1927 won over Pittsburgh Pirates, 4 games to 0
1928 won over St. Louis Cardinals, 4 games to 0

1927 Record: 110-44 (19 games ahead of Philadelphia A's)

	R*	OR	BA	HR	SB	E	CG	ShO	ERA
New York	**975**	599	**.307**	**158**	90	195	82	**11**	**3.20**
Philadelphia	841	726	.303	56	98	190	66	8	3.95
Washington	782	730	.287	29	133	195	62	10	3.95
Detroit	845	805	.289	51	**141**	206	75	5	4.12
Chicago	662	708	.278	36	90	**178**	**85**	10	3.91
Cleveland	668	766	.283	26	63	201	72	5	4.27
St. Louis	724	904	.276	55	91	248	80	4	4.95
Boston	597	856	.259	28	82	228	63	6	4.68

Top Hitters:			**Power Hitters:**		HR	RBI
	Lou Gehrig	.373		Babe Ruth	60	164
	Babe Ruth	.356		Lou Gehrig	47	173
	Earle Combs	.356		Tony Lazzeri	18	102
	Bob Meusel	.337				
	Tony Lazzeri	.309				

		Won	Lost	ERA	Saves
Starting Pitchers:	Waite Hoyt	22	7	2.63	
	Herb Pennock	19	8	3.00	
	Urban Shocker	18	6	2.84	
	Dutch Ruether	13	6	3.38	
	George Pipgras	10	3	4.11	
Ace Relievers:	Wilcy Moore	19	7	2.28	13

* R=Runs, OR=Opponents' Runs, BA=Batting Average, HR=Home Runs, SB=Stolen Bases, E=Errors, CG=Complete Games by Starting Pitchers, ShO=Shutouts, ERA=Earned Run Average. **League leaders are shown in boldface type.**

MORDECAI PETER BROWN
(THREE-FINGERED AND MINER)

MEMBER OF CHICAGO N.L. CHAMPIONSHIP
TEAM OF 1906,'07,'08,'10. A RIGHT HANDED
PITCHER, WON 239 GAMES DURING MAJOR
LEAGUE CAREER THAT ALSO INCLUDED
ST. LOUIS AND CINCINNATI N.L. AND CLUBS
IN F.L. FIRST MAJOR LEAGUER TO PITCH
FOUR CONSECUTIVE SHUTOUTS, ACHIEVING
THIS FEAT ON JUNE 13, JUNE 25, JULY 2
AND JULY 4 IN 1908.

FRANK LEROY CHANCE

FAMOUS LEADER OF CHICAGO CUBS. WON
PENNANT WITH CUBS IN FIRST FULL SEASON
AS MANAGER IN 1906 - THAT TEAM COMPILED
116 VICTORIES UNEQUALLED IN MAJOR
LEAGUE HISTORY - ALSO WON PENNANTS
IN 1907, 08 AND 1910 AND WORLD SERIES
WINNER IN 07 AND 08. STARTED WITH
CHICAGO IN 1898. ALSO MANAGER
NEW YORK A.L. AND BOSTON A.L.

The 1906 Chicago Cubs. Front row (left to right): Carl Lundgren, Tom Walsh, Johnny Evers, Jimmy Slagle, Joe Tinker. Middle row: Doc Gessler, Jack Taylor, Harry Steinfeldt, Jim McCormick, Frank Chance, Jimmy Sheckard, Pat Moran, Wildfire Schulte. Back row: Mordecai Brown, Jack Pfiester, Solly Hofman, C. G. Williams, Orval Overall, Ed Reulbach, Johnny Kling.

2

The Winningest Team of All

The 1906 Chicago Cubs

If any team could challenge the 1927 Yankees for the number-one spot, it would be a Chicago Cub team from the turn of the century. Although not as famous as many later teams, from 1906 to 1910 the Cubs *averaged* 106 wins per season. No club has ever come close to their 1906 mark of winning more than 76% of their games with a 116-36 finish.

The Cubs were a far cry from the fence-busting Yankees. Only three Cubs managed to top the Yankees' team average of .307. In the decade of the "dead" ball, Chicago's top power hitter hit only seven home runs. But the Cubs had no equal when it came to keeping home plate free of footprints. Their pitching staff was so well stocked that in 1906 they traded away the National League's strikeout king, Fred Beebe, and never missed him. No less than five of the team's pitchers held opponents to under

two earned runs per game. When combined with the Cubs' league-leading batting average and major league record fielding percentage, it was no wonder they seldom lost.

What little fame this Chicago squad has received came from a 1910 poem by Franklin P. Adams. Reporting for the New York Giants, Adams moaned about a flawless double play combination: Tinker to Evers to Chance. Historians have found, however, that smart managing and a farm accident had more to do with the Cubs' success than this double play trio.

The farm accident had happened many years before when pitcher Mordecai Brown was a young boy. One day he caught his right hand in a corn shredder, losing one finger altogether and mangling another. Although he was hardly thrilled about the accident at the time,

19

Opposing pitchers knew they had to hurl a shutout if they expected to beat Mordecai "Three Finger" Brown in 1906. That year Brown set a National League record with a 1.04 earned run average—a mark that still stands.

it proved to be a lucky break in his baseball career. With a finger missing, Brown could throw a pitch that must have been similar to Bruce Sutter's famous split-fingered fastball. Mordecai's pitch dipped so crazily that few National League batters had a clue as to how to hit it. The Cubs wisely traded for Three Finger Brown in a 1903 deal with the St. Louis Cardinals, and the great right-hander went on to post records for stinginess that have never been equalled.

The Cubs showed even more wisdom when they moved two of their men to new positions. Frank Chance first came to the Cubs as a catcher. Discouraged by his poor showing, the tall catcher threatened to quit. The Cubs finally suggested that he try moving to first base. Although Chance squawked about it at first, he finally agreed to the move. At first base he could make better use of his speed, and he worked to become a good fielder. A tough battler who stood up to being hit by pitches five times in one game, Chance was promoted to manager in 1905. The "Peerless Leader," as he was called, led the Cubs to their greatest heights with his fielding, hitting, hustle, and drive.

Although he was one of the larger, heavier players in the league, in 1907 Frank Chance led the National League with 57 stolen bases.

In 1908 Johnny Evers' knowledge of the rule-book won the pennant for Chicago. He discovered a little-known rule about force outs and used it to rob the New York Giants of a win. That one game cost the Giants the pennant and sent Chicago back to the World Series.

The other move involved Joe Tinker, a third baseman. The 5-foot, 9-inch, 135-pounder had so much speed to go with his strong arm that he was moved to shortstop. The poor man must have grumbled about that move when he made 197 errors in his first three years at shortstop! But he finally caught on to the position and led National League shortstops in fielding for five years. Although Joe and his mates could field well, there is no evidence that they had any special talent for turning a double play.

The famous poem, however, helped both Tinker and second baseman Johnny Evers into the Hall of Fame. At 5 feet, 9 inches and 115 pounds, Evers was one of the game's tiniest players. Despite his size, he never let anyone push him around. Known as "The Crab," Evers kept up such a stream of chatter that even his own teammates couldn't stand it. Shortstop Tinker wouldn't even speak to Evers for several years, including the 1906 season. That left Johnny with plenty of time for his favorite hobby: studying the rule book.

The fame of the Tinker-to-Evers-to-Chance play was a raw deal for the so-

JOSEPH B. TINKER
FAMOUS AS A MEMBER OF ONE OF BASEBALL'S
GREATEST DOUBLE PLAY COMBINATIONS-FROM
TINKER TO EVERS TO CHANCE. A BIG LEAGUER
FROM 1902 THROUGH 1916 WITH THE CHICAGO
CUBS AND CINCINNATI REDS AND THE
CHICAGO FEDS. MANAGER CINCINNATI
1913 AND CHICAGO N.L. 1916. SHORTSTOP
ON CUBS' TEAM THAT WON PENNANTS
IN 1906,'07 '08 AND 1910.

JOHN JOSEPH EVERS
"THE TROJAN"
MIDDLE-MAN OF THE FAMOUS DOUBLE
PLAY COMBINATION OF TINKER TO EVERS
TO CHANCE. WITH THE PENNANT WINNING
CHICAGO CUBS OF 1906,-07-08-10 AND WITH
THE BOSTON BRAVES' MIRACLE TEAM OF
1914. VOTED MOST VALUABLE PLAYER IN N.L.
IN 1914. SERVED AS PLAYER, COACH AND
MANAGER IN BIG LEAGUES AND AS A SCOUT
FROM 1902 THROUGH 1934. SHARES RECORD
FOR MAKING MOST SINGLES IN FOUR
- GAME WORLD SERIES.

far unmentioned third baseman, Harry Steinfeldt. Obtained from the Reds before the start of the season, Steinfeldt could field well, had a great arm, and was twice the hitter that either Evers or Tinker were. Another trade brought Brooklyn outfielder Jimmy Sheckard, a veteran outfielder who was the first to wear sunglasses in the field. In 1902 Sheckard had won the rare double honor of leading the league in both stolen bases and home runs.

Two other standouts in the Cub line-up were catcher Johnny Kling and outfielder Wildfire Schulte. Kling was so solid on both offense and defense that Pirate great Honus Wagner named him the all-time greatest catcher. Schulte, one of the few players of his time who refused to choke up on the bat, could hit with power.

On any other club, pitchers such as Ed Reulbach, Jack Pfeister, or Orval Overall could have been top starters. But as good as they were, they were all still outshown by Three Finger Brown.

New York's Christy Matthewson fired three shutouts in the 1905 World Series. Thanks to the Cubs, it wasn't until 1911 that baseball's most dominating pitcher made another World Series appearance.

In 1906 Chicago faced stiff competition from both the New York Giants and the Pittsburgh Pirates. With the great Wagner at shortstop, Pittsburgh was always a threat. The Cubs, though, were more concerned about the New York club, which had won the last two pennants. With hurlers like Christy Matthewson and Iron Man McGinnity, the Giants believed their pitching staff was as good as the Cubs.

Through the months of April and May, Chicago and New York waged a hot battle for the lead. The best duel in sports at the time may have been the pitching contests between Matthewson and Brown. Three Finger was in the middle of a nine-game winning streak against Matthewson, and he did not lose to him in 1906. With another Giant-killer, Jack Pfeister, putting his hex on New York, the Cubs began to pull away. They breezed through August with a 26-3 mark to leave the Giants far behind.

Manager John McGraw and his Giants must have wondered what was happening to baseball. They won 96 and lost 56 in 1906, a record good enough to win the pennant most years. Yet they finished a full *20* games behind Chicago.

The Cubs dominated all areas of the game. They scored far more runs than anyone else (704) and allowed far fewer (381). With Steinfeldt hitting .327; Chance, .319; and Kling, .312, Chicago topped the league in batting with a .262 mark. The unsung Steinfeldt also led the National League in runs batted in, while Chance took the honors in stolen bases.

With a major league record .969 fielding percentage and a flawless pitching staff, the Cubs had more than enough offense. Their hurlers chalked up 28 shutouts, including nine 1-0 wins. Ten of their shutouts belonged to Three Finger Brown. Brown earned his 26-6 record with an earned run average of 1.04, a National League record that has stood for over 75 years. Following the lead of their ace, Ed Reulbach went 20-4 with a 1.65 ERA, and Pfeister, 19-9 with 1.56. While only two other National League pitchers held foes to fewer than two earned runs per game, the entire Cub staff posted a 1.76 ERA!

Baseball was treated to a rare, one-city World Series that year when the Cubs took on their crosstown rivals, the White Sox. Known as the Hitless Wonders, the White Sox had won the American League pennant despite finishing last in batting with a .230 average! Fans who enjoy slugfests would have been bored by the Series. There were no home runs, and neither team batted over .200.

The Chicago teams were tied at two wins each when the Cubs made an all-out effort to win game five. Reulbach, Pfeister, and Overall all pitched, but the Cubs still lost. That meant the Cubs had to turn to Brown. Since no travel days were needed for the Series, the games were played on consecutive days. That was bad news for the overworked Brown, who had thrown 18 innings in the last five days. His arm was worn out for game six, and the Cubs were upset by the Hitless Wonders.

But the Cubs proved the loss to be a fluke. They swept to easy World Series wins during the next two years and built the best five-year mark in baseball history. Cub fans who suffered through nearly 40 years—until 1984—without a pennant may have found it hard to believe that there was a time when the Chicago Cubs were the class act of major league ball.

The Cubs take batting practice before game three of the 1906 World Series. They didn't take enough, however, as the White Sox' Ed Walsh shut them out, 3 to 0.

THE 1906 CHICAGO CUBS

Dynasty Years: 1906-1908

World Series Record:

1906 lost to Chicago White Sox, 4 games to 2
1907 won over Detroit Tigers, 4 games to 1
1908 won over Detroit Tigers, 4 games to 1

1906 Record: 116-36 (20 games ahead of the New York Giants)

	R*	OR	BA	HR	SB	E	CG	ShO	ERA
Chicago	**704**	**381**	**.262**	20	283	**194**	125	28	**1.76**
New York	625	508	.255	15	**288**	233	105	16	2.49
Pittsburgh	622	464	.261	12	162	228	116	26	2.21
Philadelphia	530	568	.241	12	180	271	108	20	2.58
Brooklyn	495	620	.236	**25**	175	283	119	22	3.13
Cincinnati	530	582	.238	16	170	262	126	11	2.69
St. Louis	475	620	.235	10	110	272	118	4	3.04
Boston	408	646	.226	l6	93	337	137	10	3.17

				HR	RBI
Top Hitters: Harry Steinfeldt	.327	**Power Hitters:** Wildfire Schulte		7	60
Frank Chance	.319	Harry Steinfeldt		7	60
Johnny Kling	.312				
Wildfire Schulte	.282				

		Won	Lost	ERA
Starting Pitchers:	Mordecai Brown	26	6	1.04
	Jack Pfeister	20	8	1.56
	Ed Reulbach	20	4	1.65
	Carl Lundgren	17	6	2.21
	Jack Taylor	12	3	1.83
	Orval Overall	12	3	1.83

Ace Relievers: NONE

* R=Runs, OR=Opponents' Runs, BA=Batting Average, HR=Home Runs, SB=Stolen Bases, E=Errors, CG=Complete Games by Starting Pitchers, ShO=Shutouts, ERA=Earned Run Average. **League leaders are shown in boldface type.**

Right: The Big Red Machine's batting order was virtually a maintenance-free unit, but the pitching staff required continual fine tuning from manager Sparky "Captain Hook" Anderson.

Below: The 1976 Cincinnati Reds. Front row (left to right): Pete Rose, Joe Morgan, Coach Russ Nixon, Coach Ted Kluszewski, Coach Larry Shepard, Manager Sparky Anderson, Coach George Scherger, Fred Norman, Doug Flynn, Manny Sarmiento. Middle row: Bernie Stowe (equipment manager), Paul Campbell (traveling secretary), Joel Youngblood, Don Gullett, Ed Armbrister, George Foster, Tony Perez, Johnny Bench, Ken Griffey, Will McEnaney, Dan Driessen, Mark Stowe (bat boy). Back row: Bob Bailey, Dave Concepción, Gary Nolan, Bill Plummer, Pat Zachry, Santo Alcala, Jack Billingham, Rawley Eastwick, Cesar Geronimo, Pedro Borbon, Mike Lum.

★★★ 3 ★★★

Man vs. Machine

The 1976 Cincinnati Reds

Cincinnati's Big Red Machine was sputtering worse than an ancient tractor. The once-promising team of the early 1970s had faded without winning a World Series. In 1973 they had been bounced out of the playoffs by an unimpressive New York Mets team, and the next year they failed to win their division. Continuing their slide in the first month and a half of the 1975 season, the Reds had lost more games than they had won.

Manager Sparky Anderson puzzled over the problem and saw only one glaring weakness: third base. For a moment, he dreamed about putting Pete Rose there. Naw, Rose was happy in left field. He had hated it when the Reds had tried to make a third baseman out of him back in the 1960s. You can't just move a big star like Rose. "Well, what would it hurt to ask?" thought Sparky.

No sooner did the manager bring up

the subject than Rose headed for the infield to practice fielding ground balls. By doing so, he helped work out the last mechanical difficulty in the Big Red Machine. The Reds went on to win 90 of their last 125 games to finish 20 games ahead of the defending division champ, the Los Angeles Dodgers. In a thrilling World Series, they claimed their championship by beating Boston. 1975 may have been an exciting year for the Reds, but it was only a warmup for what would be the hardest hitting lineup in modern baseball: the 1976 Reds.

The 1976 Reds completed a patient building project that had begun back in 1960. That year Cincinnati had signed Pete Rose, a switch-hitting jack-of-all-trades, who had become legendary for his hustle. Collecting hits faster than any big league player since Stan "The Man" Musial, Rose hovered near the top

Pete Rose, alias "Charlie Hustle," cranks up the Big Red Machine with a patented line drive.

of the batting race almost every year. In that same 1960 season, the Reds had signed a powerful Cuban, Atanasio "Tony" Perez. The right-handed slugger came through so often with runners on base that he had become the Reds' all-time leading RBI man.

It wasn't until five years later that Cincinnati scouts unearthed another super player. That year they used their number-two draft choice to select an Oklahoman named Johnny Bench. The Reds moved Bench from the mound to behind the plate, and he developed beyond their wildest dreams. Breaking in with Cincinnati in 1968, he won Rookie of the Year honors. Two years later, he added the Most Valuable Player Trophy to his collection. Bench's slingshot throwing arm helped him win 10 straight Golden Glove awards for defensive play. At the same time, he socked more home runs than any other catcher in major league history.

Rose, Perez, and Bench formed the backbone of a team that was good, but not great, in the early 1970s. The second stage of construction was boosted by the arrival of general manager Robert Howsam from St. Louis in 1967. With a keen eye for talent, Howsam's organization was able to make good with number-one draft choices such as Don Gullett. Sometimes they could even spot a gem, such as speedy outfielder Ken Griffey, a 29th round pick, in the later rounds.

Howsam's greatest skill, however, was in trading. There were two deals in which he picked clean his National League rivals. The first seemed like a minor trade in 1971. The Reds traded shortstop Frank Duffy and pitcher Vern Geishert to San Francisco for reserve outfielder George Foster. The slow-developing Foster soon turned the trade into a steal, however. By 1975 he was quickly becoming the most feared Reds hitter of all. His surprising home-run power had pushed the Reds into clearing a space for him in left field, which is why Rose ended up at third base.

The second trade was a massive deal that nearly got Howsam run out of

Every season from 1967 to 1976, Tony Perez drove in 90 or more runs for the Reds. The trade that sent him to Montreal following the 1976 season helped to pull the plug on the Red's dynasty.

George Foster (left) and Joe Morgan (right) collected the hardware for the Reds in 1976. Foster won the National League's RBI trophy, and Morgan was voted its Most Valuable Player.

town by angered fans. He swapped slugger Lee May, second baseman Tommy Helms, and reserve Jimmy Stewart for troublesome Joe Morgan and four others. The trade was expected to help Houston win the pennant. It did not, and, in the end, it was the Reds who came away grinning. Morgan, a 5-foot, 7-inch second baseman, turned out to be a team leader as well as one of the most complete players in the game. His many walks and stolen bases made him a pitcher's

pest, and he could hit for power as well as average. Along with Morgan came a good pitcher, Jack Billingham, and Cesar Geronimo, an excellent defensive center fielder.

Cincinnati's farm system completed the lineup when it turned out shortstop Dave Concepción. By 1975 Dave had established himself as an all-star at that position.

With such a fast, talented, and powerful lineup, the Reds could hardly wait for 1976 to begin. Their one worry was their starting pitching. Talented throwers like Gary Nolan and Don Gullett rarely got through an injury-free season, but Manager Anderson also hoped to get good performances out of Billingham, Fred Norman, and rookie Pat Zachry. If not, Sparky had learned how to survive by using his bullpen. Changing pitchers so often that he earned the name "Captain Hook," Sparky outlasted foes with an endless parade of relief men. In 1976 he could count on Pedro Borbon and last year's rookie sensations, Rawley Eastwick and Will McEnaney.

The Dodgers hoped to challenge the Big Red Machine, but they never had a chance. The Reds simply pounded opponents out of the park with their hitting. Morgan was enjoying another super year, and his only competition for the Most Valuable Player Award was teammate Foster. The weakest links in the lineup turned out to be Tony Perez and Johnny Bench, and not many pitchers breathed a sigh of relief when those two came to bat.

When the pitching staff needed some patchwork, Borbon and Eastwick combined to pitch in 140 games, with East-wick collecting a league-leading 26 saves. Pat Zachry came through with 14 wins to win a share of the National League Rookie of the Year title. None of the starters had more than 15 wins, yet the Reds won their division easily.

Looking at the Reds' batting totals for the year, they could have done well in the standings with even a minor league pitching staff. They led both leagues in team average, home runs, triples, doubles, and runs. Buried under the mound of offensive titles was the fact that Cincinnati fielded better than anyone else. Rose, Bench, Geronimo, Concepción, and Morgan all were among the best at manning their spots. Reds' starters also combined to steal an impressive 186 bases.

The big challenge for the Reds was supposed to come in the play-offs, where they faced Philadelphia. Led by stars like Steve Carlton and Mike Schmidt, the Phils had finished the regular season with nearly the same record as the Reds: 101-61 to the Reds' 102-60. But the Phils were mere men up against a machine. The Reds coasted to two wins and then roared from behind to overhaul the Phils in the ninth inning of game three.

Winning the World Series wasn't as tough as Pete Rose makes it look here as he slides into third base. The Reds walked all over the Yankees by scores of 5-1, 4-3, 6-2, and 7-2.

In the World Series, the free-agent-rich Yankees stood in the way of another title. But they were no match for the Big Red Machine, particularly Johnny Bench. Rebounding from his poor season, Bench hit .533, smacked two homers in one game, and kept Yankee runners from stealing bases. Cincinnati won all four games by a combined score of 22-8, the first consecutive Series win by a National League team since 1922.

The Reds had also become the first team to breeze through the play-offs and the World Series without a loss. Had the Mets' great pitcher, Tom Seaver, joined them that season instead of the next, the Reds might well be considered in the same class as the 1927 Yankees. As it was, without a single outstanding, healthy starting pitcher, they had still overwhelmed the best that baseball could offer that year.

THE 1976 CINCINNATI REDS

Dynasty Years: 1975, 1976

Play-off Record:
1975 won over Pittsburgh Pirates, 3 games to 0
1976 won over Philadelphia Phillies, 3 games to 0

World Series Record:
1975 won over Boston Red Sox, 4 games to 3
1976 won over New York Yankees, 4 games to 0

1976 Record: 102-60 (10 games ahead of Los Angeles Dodgers)

	R*	OR	BA	HR	SB	E	CG	ShO	ERA
Cincinnati	**857**	633	**.280**	**141**	210	102	33	12	3.51
Philadelphia	770	557	.272	110	127	115	34	9	3.10
Pittsburgh	708	630	.267	110	130	163	45	12	3.37
Los Angeles	608	543	.251	91	144	128	47	17	3.02
New York	615	**538**	.246	102	66	131	**53**	**18**	**2.94**
Houston	625	657	.256	66	150	140	42	17	3.56
Chicago	611	728	.251	105	74	140	27	12	3.93
San Francisco	595	686	.246	85	88	186	27	18	3.53
San Diego	570	662	.247	64	92	141	47	11	3.65
St. Louis	629	671	.260	63	123	174	35	15	3.61
Atlanta	620	700	.245	82	74	167	33	13	3.86
Montreal	531	734	.235	94	86	155	26	10	3.99

Top Hitters:			**Power Hitters:**		HR	RBI
	Ken Griffey	.336		George Foster	29	121
	Pete Rose	.323		Joe Morgan	27	111
	Joe Morgan	.320		Tony Perez	19	91
	Cesar Geronimo	.307		Johnny Bench	16	74
	George Foster	.306				
	Dave Concepción	.281				

		Won	Lost	ERA	Saves
Starting Pitchers:	Gary Nolan	15	9	3.46	
	Pat Zachry	14	7	2.74	
	Fred Norman	12	7	3.10	
	Jack Billingham	12	10	4.32	
	Don Gullett	11	3	3.00	
Ace Relievers:	Rawley Eastwick	11	5	2.08	26
	Pedro Borbon	4	3	3.35	8

* R=Runs, OR=Opponents' Runs, BA=Batting Average, HR=Home Runs, SB=Stolen Bases, E=Errors, CG=Complete Games by Starting Pitchers, ShO=Shutouts, ERA=Earned Run Average. **League leaders are shown in boldface type.**

FRANK ROBINSON
CINCINNATI N.L., BALTIMORE A.L.,
LOS ANGELES N.L., CALIFORNIA A.L.,
CLEVELAND A.L., 1956-1976
FIRST TO BE CHOSEN MOST VALUABLE PLAYER
IN BOTH LEAGUES -- N.L. IN 1961 AND A.L.
IN 1966. SET RECORDS BY HITTING HOMERS
IN 32 DIFFERENT PARKS AND WITH PAIR OF
GRAND-SLAMMERS IN SUCCESSIVE INNINGS IN
1970. FOURTH IN HOMERS (586), FIFTH IN
EXTRA BASES ON LONG HITS (2,430), SIXTH
IN TOTAL BASES (5,373) ON RETIRING. LED
N.L. IN SLUGGING PCT. IN 1960-61-62 AND
A.L. IN BATTING, HOMERS, RUNS BATTED IN,
TOTAL BASES AND SLUGGING PCT. IN 1966.

BROOKS CALBERT ROBINSON, JR.
BALTIMORE A.L. 1955-1977
ESTABLISHED MODERN STANDARD OF EXCELLENCE
FOR THIRD BASEMEN, SETTING MAJOR LEAGUE
RECORDS AT HIS POSITION FOR SEASONS (23),
FIELDING PCT. (.971), GAMES (2,870), PUTOUTS
(2,697), ASSISTS (6,205), AND DOUBLE PLAYS (618),
HIT 268 CAREER HOME RUNS. NAMED TO 18
CONSECUTIVE ALL STAR TEAMS. MVP OF 1970
WORLD SERIES. AMERICAN LEAGUE MVP IN 1964.

The 1970 Baltimore Orioles. Front: Jay Mazzone (batboy). Front row (left to right): Tom Phoebus, Don Buford, Coach Jim Frey, Coach Bill Hunter, Manager Earl Weaver, Coach George Bamberger, Coach George Staller, Dave McNally, Chico Salmon. Middle row: Andy Etchebarren, Boog Powell, Pete Richert, Mark Belanger, Dave Leonhard, Brooks Robinson, Ellie Hendricks, Merv Rettenmund, Dave Johnson, Eddie Watt. Back row: Marcelino Lopez, Jim Palmer, Moe Drabowsky, Frank Robinson, Mike Cuellar, Dick Hall, Bobby Grich, Curt Motton, Terry Crowley, Paul Blair.

4

When the American League Was Bird Feed

The 1970 Baltimore Orioles

The Baltimore Oriole farm system has long been known as the American League's pitching factory. Young hurlers have come up to help the Birds lead the league in ERA so often that it is as if they have discovered a secret formula for pitching success. In the 1960s, the Orioles' minor league teams came through with a more complete line of baseball products, and Baltimore was able to custom build a dream team from the large selection of homegrown hitters and fielders. These players carried the Orioles to five American League East pennants in six years, three straight seasons with more than 100 wins, and three straight World Series appearances. Perhaps no team has ever had such an even blend of pitching, hitting, and fielding as the 1970 Orioles.

Although Baltimore developed most of its own players, they could not have reached greatness without a couple of late arrivals from the National League. We have seen the Reds pull off slick deals to build their team, but in 1965 they got burned. Someone in the Cincinnati organization decided that Frank Robinson was getting old. Although Frank was only 30 and could still match his main rivals, Willie Mays and Hank Aaron, he was sent packing to the Orioles for the modest price of pitcher Milt Pappas.

The "aging" Robinson celebrated the trade by leading his new league in home runs, average, and RBIs in 1966! Along with his skill, Robinson had a way of firing up his team. He received credit for inspiring the Birds to their 1966 upset sweep of the Dodgers. Fresh from a .308 average and 32 home runs the previous year, Frank was showing no signs of falling apart in 1970.

Five years after he was declared "too old" by the Reds, a frisky Frank Robinson still led the Oriole offense.

Baltimore's second break came in 1968 at the expense of the luckless Houston Astros. Houston could not be blamed for giving up on screwball specialist Mike Cuellar. After all, the lefty had won only 8 games while losing 11 for them in 1967. Before that, he had done little to earn his keep at Cincinnati and St. Louis. No sooner did Cuellar land in Baltimore, however, than he turned into a regular 20-game winner.

At least part of Cuellar's new success must have been due to the glove work of his new teammates. If an Oriole pitcher could keep the ball in the park, there was a good chance that someone could catch it. One opponent claimed that hitting a ball through the left side of the Oriole infield was like trying to throw hamburger through a wall. There was no point in hitting anything near third base. There Brooks Robinson was in the middle of a 23-year career of taking hits away from batters. Winner of 11 fielding titles in his career, Robinson's quick reactions helped him to play the position better than anyone had before.

Brooks, "the other Robinson," would have made a splendid hockey goalie. Here he makes another save, stealing a base hit from his opponent.

Prospects for a hit weren't much better for a ball aimed to the shortstop. Mark Belanger had taken over the job from the league's top shortstop, Luis Aparicio, in 1968 and did it so well that no one noticed the difference. The third spectacular fielder, Paul Blair, patrolled center field. Starting with his rookie season of 1965, his range, acrobatic catches, and strong arm had been the talk of the league.

Left fielder Frank Robinson and second baseman Dave Johnson were no slouches with the glove, either. And it surprised many fans to learn that huge first baseman Boog Powell was well above average at his position, too. The ex-football tackle was so powerful that many assumed he was in the lineup only for his batting. But as his fellow infielders knew, there were few better at digging low throws out of the dirt.

On offense, Baltimore manager Earl Weaver liked to play for the big inning. Instead of scratching out runs with sacrifice bunts, hit-and-runs, and steals,

Manager Earl Weaver wasn't the easiest person to get along with. It was a toss-up as to whether he argued more with umpires . . .

Weaver counted on "Dr. Longball." Powell and Frank Robinson came through with the most home runs, with each good for around 30 per season. But Brooks Robinson, Paul Blair, and second baseman Johnson could also reach the fences. Even the leadoff batter, chunky, 5-foot, 7-inch Don Buford, hit with power. A fine hitter who also walked often, Buford hit into fewer double plays per at bat than anyone in the game's history.

This combination of offense and defense made life comfortable for the mound crew. Cuellar rebounded from his 8-11 season at Houston to post a 23-11 mark in 1969. Joining him as baseball's top left-handed duo was strikeout pitcher Dave McNally, and hard throwing Jim Palmer provided the right-handed pitching. After arm injuries in 1967, Palmer's career had seemed over. Baltimore even left him open to the expansion draft, but no one wanted him. Palmer had recovered, though, and was on his way to winning three Cy Young Awards as the league's top pitcher.

Baltimore's bullpen was like the rest of the team: balanced. When the Orioles needed right-handed relief, they called

... or with star pitcher Jim Palmer. The feud, however, never stopped either Palmer or Weaver from winning.

on Eddie Watt. If a lefty was called for, Pet Richert could do the job.

Baseball had split into four divisions in 1969, but it was not until 1972 that the American League East had its first divisional race. The 1970 Orioles roared through the schedule without a challenge. When Weaver asked for Dr. Longball, he often got it. Seven of the eight starters smacked 10 or more homers.

Boog Powell enjoyed his finest year, winning the American League Most Valuable Player Award. His .297 average, 35 home runs, and 114 RBIs had helped him earn that prize. Frank Robinson added yet another year of embarrassment for the Reds with .306 and 25 home runs. Brooks Robinson clouted 18 homers, and the speedy Blair-Buford outfield combination teamed up for 35 more. Even though no one was in the top two in any major offensive category, with contributions from all its players, the Orioles led the league in runs.

As usual, the Birds topped the league in ERA with 3.15. Led by Cuellar at 24-8 and McNally at 24-9, all three of the top starters broke into the 20-win column. Jim Palmer was the "hard luck" pitcher of the staff, notching only 20 wins against 10 losses with his sparkling 2.71 ERA. As usual, the bullpen balanced the scales with 13 saves from Richert and 12 from Watt.

Baltimore finished with 108 wins and 54 losses to coast in a full 15 games ahead of the pack. That brought their two-year total to 217 wins, easily an American League record. Baltimore then moved into the play-offs, determined to make up for their 1969 upset loss to the Mets. First they sent the Minnesota Twins scattering for cover, scoring 27 runs in a three-game sweep to the pennant. Then it was on to the World Series to face the Reds.

In the Series, the Orioles pounded out 10 of Weaver's beloved home runs and left the rest to Brooks Robinson's magical glove. To go along with his .429 average, Brooks made at least four plays in the Series that were beyond belief. The frustrated Reds were never able to get into the groove, and Baltimore won, four games to one.

A team with talent spread throughout its 25-man roster, the well-balanced Orioles were truly a manager's dream. Had they enjoyed the same success in their other World Series ventures, they might have gained more fame.

THE 1970 BALTIMORE ORIOLES

Dynasty Years: 1969-1971

Play-off Record:

1969 won over Minnesota Twins, 3 games to 0
1970 won over Minnesota Twins, 3 games to 0
1971 won over Oakland A's, 3 games to 0

World Series Record:

1969 lost to New York Mets, 4 games to 1
1970 won over Cincinnati Reds, 4 games to 1
1971 lost to Pittsburgh Pirates, 4 games to 3

1970 Record: 108-54 (15 games ahead of New York Yankees)

	R*	OR	BA	HR	SB	E	CG	ShO	ERA
Baltimore	**792**	**574**	.257	179	84	117	**60**	12	**3.15**
Minnesota	744	605	**.262**	153	57	123	26	12	3.23
New York	680	612	.251	111	105	130	36	6	3.25
Oakland	678	593	.249	171	**131**	141	33	**15**	3.30
Boston	786	722	.262	**203**	50	156	38	8	3.90
California	631	630	.251	114	69	127	21	10	3.48
Detroit	666	731	.238	148	29	133	33	9	4.09
Cleveland	649	675	.249	183	25	133	34	8	3.91
Washington	626	689	.238	138	72	**116**	20	11	3.80
Kansas City	611	705	.244	97	97	152	30	11	3.78
Milwaukee	613	751	.242	126	91	136	31	2	4.20
Chicago	633	822	.253	123	54	165	20	6	4.54

Top Hitters:	
Merv Rettenmund	.322
Frank Robinson	.306
Boog Powell	.297
Dave Johnson	.281
Brooks Robinson	.276

Power Hitters:		HR	RBI
Boog Powell		35	114
Frank Robinson		25	78
Brooks Robinson		18	94
Paul Blair		18	65
Merv Rettenmund		18	58
Don Buford		17	66

Starting Pitchers:	Won	Lost	ERA	Saves
Mike Cuellar	24	8	3.47	
Dave McNally	24	9	3.22	
Jim Palmer	20	10	2.71	
Jim Hardin	6	5	3.54	
Tom Phoebus	5	5	3.07	

Ace Relievers:	Won	Lost	ERA	Saves
Pete Richert	7	2	1.96	13
Eddie Watt	7	7	3.27	12
Dick Hall	10	5	3.10	3

* R=Runs, OR=Opponents' Runs, BA=Batting Average, HR=Home Runs, SB=Stolen Bases, E=Errors, CG=Complete Games by Starting Pitchers, ShO=Shutouts, ERA=Earned Run Average. **League leaders are shown in boldface type.**

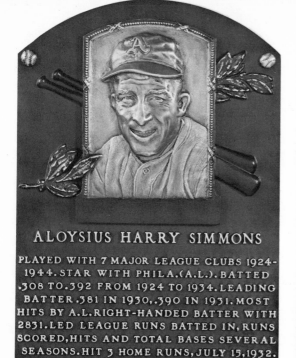

ALOYSIUS HARRY SIMMONS

PLAYED WITH 7 MAJOR LEAGUE CLUBS 1924-
1944. STAR WITH PHILA. (A.L.). BATTED
.308 TO .392 FROM 1924 TO 1934. LEADING
BATTER .381 IN 1930, .390 IN 1931. MOST
HITS BY A.L. RIGHT-HANDED BATTER WITH
2831. LED LEAGUE RUNS BATTED IN, RUNS
SCORED, HITS AND TOTAL BASES SEVERAL
SEASONS. HIT 3 HOME RUNS, JULY 15, 1932.
LIFETIME BATTING AVERAGE .334.

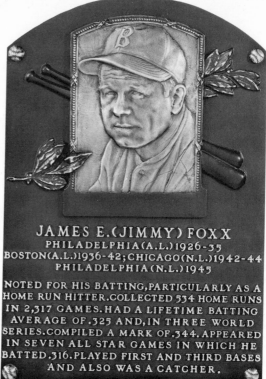

JAMES E. (JIMMY) FOXX

PHILADELPHIA (A.L.) 1926-35
BOSTON (A.L.) 1936-42; CHICAGO (N.L.) 1942-44
PHILADELPHIA (N.L.) 1945

NOTED FOR HIS BATTING, PARTICULARLY AS A
HOME RUN HITTER. COLLECTED 534 HOME RUNS
IN 2,317 GAMES. HAD A LIFETIME BATTING
AVERAGE OF .325 AND, IN THREE WORLD
SERIES, COMPILED A MARK OF .344. APPEARED
IN SEVEN ALL STAR GAMES IN WHICH HE
BATTED .316. PLAYED FIRST AND THIRD BASES
AND ALSO WAS A CATCHER.

The 1931 Philadelphia A's. Front row (left to right): Mickey Cochrane, Jimmy Dykes, Eddie Collins, not known, Connie Mack, Eberling, Al Simmons, Mule Haas, Eric McNair, Doc Cramer. Middle row: Eddie Rommel, Phil Todt, Hank McDonald, Rube Walberg, Lefty Grove, not known, Dib Williams, Bing Miller, Jim Peterson, Jimmy Foxx. Back row: Earl Mack, Lew Krausse, Max Bishop, Waite Hoyt, Johnnie Heving, Roy Mahaffey, Joe Palmissno, Gleason, Jim Moore, Joe Boley.

5

Too Good for Their Own Good?

The 1931 Philadelphia Athletics

You have to wonder about including in this book a team that could not even impress its own manager. Connie Mack, owner and manager of the Philadelphia A's, always insisted that his 1929-31 teams were not as good as his 1910-14 teams. Perhaps Mr. Mack just had a fondness for the good old days. But a 1963 survey of the American Academy of Sports Editors named the '29-31 version of the A's as the second best team in baseball history, second to the 1927 Yankees. The A's were overwhelming in all three seasons of that dynasty, but we'll highlight 1931, the year in which their two greatest stars shone the brightest.

Those who claim that the spending wars brought on by free agency in the 1970s are a new danger to the game would do well to study the history of the Philadelphia A's. Their many ups and downs can be traced to one cause: money.

Between 1910 and 1914, Philadelphia built one of the American League's first great teams. Led by pitchers Chief Bender and Ed Plank and the "$100,000 infield," the A's won three World Series. But when a new league threatened to start bidding wars for players in 1915, owner Mack bailed out. Within two years, most of his team had been traded or sold. The A's plunged to the bottom of the standings and stayed there for seven years. Their struggles continued until Mack opened his wallet again in 1924.

It must have been painful for the thrifty Mack to hand over $50,000 for the contract of a Milwaukee youngster, Aloysius Szymanski. Better known as Al Simmons, the lad had a strange habit of stepping away from the plate when he swung. "Bucketfoot Al" worked himself into a rage before hitting and took it out on the pitcher. Simmons hit for a .334 life-

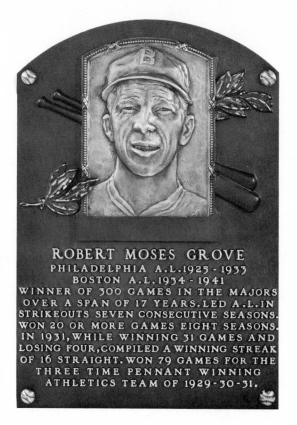

ROBERT MOSES GROVE
PHILADELPHIA A.L. 1925 - 1933
BOSTON A.L. 1934 - 1941
WINNER OF 300 GAMES IN THE MAJORS
OVER A SPAN OF 17 YEARS. LED A.L. IN
STRIKEOUTS SEVEN CONSECUTIVE SEASONS.
WON 20 OR MORE GAMES EIGHT SEASONS.
IN 1931, WHILE WINNING 31 GAMES AND
LOSING FOUR, COMPILED A WINNING STREAK
OF 16 STRAIGHT. WON 79 GAMES FOR THE
THREE TIME PENNANT WINNING
ATHLETICS TEAM OF 1929-30-31.

Cornelius McGillicuddy, better known as Connie Mack, owned and managed the Philadelphia A's for 50 years. Throughout his career, he fought a constant battle between his checkbook and his desire to win.

time average with 307 home runs and drove in more than 100 runs in 11 straight seasons.

Mack had to dig even deeper—into the $100,000 range—to sign pitcher Robert Moses "Lefty" Grove in 1925. Although many considered Grove to be the top pitcher in baseball in the early 1920s, Lefty had stayed with the well-paying, minor league Baltimore Orioles for four seasons.

At the same time, they lured Grove to Philadelphia, the A's bid $50,000 for

GORDON "MICKEY" COCHRANE
PHILADELPHIA A.L.1925 - 1933
DETROIT A.L.1934 - 1937
FIERY CATCHER COMPILED A NOTABLE
RECORD BOTH AS A PLAYER AND MANAGER.
THE SPARK OF THE ATHLETICS' CHAMPIONSHIP
TEAMS OF 1929-30-31, HAD AN AVERAGE
BATTING MARK OF .346 FOR THOSE THREE
YEARS. LED DETROIT TO TWO LEAGUE
CHAMPIONSHIPS AND A WORLD SERIES
TITLE IN 1935.

because with them on, he could see Foxx too clearly. "Double X" hit 534 homers in his career, including 58 in 1932.

With those four Hall of Famers on the field, the A's needed little else to become a winner. But they were also blessed

Called by some sportswriters as the "right-handed Babe Ruth," Jimmy Foxx won or shared four American League home-run titles.

catcher Mickey Cochrane. Cochrane, the "shortstop in shinpads," was a battler and a team leader. A five-sport star at Boston University, Mickey could play any position on the field. Cochrane, considered one of the top catchers of all time, earned a lifetime average of .320.

The fourth cornerstone to the team was Jimmy Foxx. Foxx signed with the A's at the age of 17 and displayed his large muscles by cutting off the sleeves of his shirts. Yankee pitcher Lefty Gomez once said he gave up wearing glasses with a good supporting cast, including two workhorse pitchers. Six-foot, four-inch George Earnshaw was after his third-straight 20-win season in 1931. With Lefty Rube Walberg, the A's had three solid starters who could be counted on for over 800 innings of work.

Philadelphia's outfield included speedy Mule Haas and veteran Bing Miller, one of the most difficult batters to strike out. The infield was in the capable hands of such men as Max Bishop, known as Camera Eye for his knowledge of the strike zone. Jimmy Dykes provided laughs as well as good play at third base. During a World Series rally, Dykes got so excited that he knocked the respected Mr. Mack off the bench!

The A's easily won the American League pennant in both 1929 and 1930 and took the World Series both years. In 1931 they set out to be the first team to take three straight World Series titles. The first part of the job came easily as they again coasted to a pennant. The fact that they left Ruth, Gehrig, and the rest of the Yanks in the dust for three straight years gives an idea of how well they played.

Simmons bounced back from a spring contract squabble to lead the league with a solid .390 average. Bucketfoot Al also drilled 22 home runs and drove in 128 runs. Pushed by the Yankees' young catching star Bill Dickey, Mickey Cochrane hit .349 with 17 homers. Foxx went through the kind of "off year" that most players only dream of: .291 with 30 home runs and 120 RBIs.

Philadelphia's three starting pitchers hogged most of the mound work that season. Each of them worked over 280 innings and showed no signs of tiring. Earnshaw posted a 21-7 mark, and Walberg was 20-12. But the main reason the A's destroyed the Yankees was the left arm of Robert Grove. Had the A's scored just nine more timely runs for him, Grove's record would have been 35-0! Lefty won 16 in a row at one point and lost his try for number 17 by a score of 1-0. (The winning run scored on a dropped ball by one of his fielders.) A grim competitor with a nasty temper, Grove threw a tantrum in the locker room after the game.

Lefty was so far beyond his rivals that year that he seemed to belong in another league. Besides his 31-4 record, Grove picked up five saves working in relief.

The four games he lost were by scores of 2-1, 7-5, 1-0 and 4-3. At a time of heavy hitting, when teams averaged more than five runs per game, Grove kept his ERA at 2.06.

With Grove in charge, Philadelphia rolled to its best mark ever: 107 wins and 45 losses. Then it was off to the World Series and the goal of three straight championships. The A's would have

Al Simmons (right) breaks up a one-hitter by spitbal specialist Burleigh Grimes with this ninth-inning home run in the 1931 World Series.

With four doubles, a home run, five stolen bases, and flawless fielding, Cardinal center fielder Pepper Martin (batting) almost singlehandedly destroyed Philadelphia's bid for a third straight World Series win.

made it if it hadn't been for the "Wild Horse of the Osage," Pepper Martin. The Cardinal rookie ran wild in the series with hits, base running, and fielding. Martin collected 12 hits in his first 18 at bats to help St. Louis win three of the first six games.

It was Earnshaw's turn to start the final game, but he could not match his previous outings. Still the A's threatened to win on a great ninth inning rally. It fell short, however, when Pepper Martin made a difficult catch for the final out.

Despite such legendary World Series rallies and the 1929 game in which they overcame an 8-0 score with 10 runs in the seventh, the A's apparently had taken some of the excitement out of the game. According to Connie Mack, Philadelphia wins had become so routine that fans didn't bother to come and watch them anymore. Always one with an eye on high player salaries, Connie Mack broke up his great team after the 1932 season. Again the A's fell to the low end of the standings, and they never again came close to matching the 1931 champs who were "too good for their own good."

THE 1931 PHILADELPHIA A'S

Dynasty Years: 1929-1931

World Series Record:

1929 won over Chicago Cubs, 4 games to 1
1930 won over St. Louis Cardinals, 4 games to 2
1931 lost to St. Louis Cardinals, 4 games to 3

1931 Record: 107-45 (13.5 games ahead of New York Yankees)

	R*	OR	BA	HR	SB	E	CG	ShO	ERA
Philadelphia	858	**626**	.287	118	27	**141**	97	12	**3.47**
New York	**1067**	760	**.297**	155	138	169	78	4	4.20
Washington	843	691	.285	49	72	142	60	6	3.76
Cleveland	885	833	.296	71	63	232	76	6	4.63
St. Louis	722	870	.271	76	73	232	65	4	4.76
Boston	625	800	.262	37	43	188	61	5	4.60
Detroit	651	836	.268	43	117	220	93	5	4.56
Chicago	704	939	.260	27	94	245	54	6	5.05

Top Hitters:			**Power Hitters:**		HR	RBI
	Al Simmons	.390		Jimmy Foxx	30	120
	Mickey Cochrane	.349		Al Simmons	22	128
	Mule Haas	.323		Mickey Cochrane	17	89
	Max Bishop	.294				
	Jimmy Foxx	.291				
	Bing Miller	.281				

Starting Pitchers:		Won	Lost	ERA
	Lefty Grove	31	4	2.06
	George Earnshaw	21	7	3.67
	Rube Walberg	20	12	3.74
	Roy Mahaffey	15	4	4.21
	Waite Hoyt	10	5	4.22
	Eddie Rommel	7	5	2.97

Ace Relievers: NONE

---

* R=Runs, OR=Opponents' Runs, BA=Batting Average, HR=Home Runs, SB=Stolen Bases, E=Errors, CG=Complete Games by Starting Pitchers, ShO=Shutouts, ERA=Earned Run Average. **League leaders are shown in boldface type.**

MICKEY CHARLES MANTLE
NEW YORK A.L. 1951-1968
HIT 536 HOME RUNS. WON LEAGUE HOMER TITLE
AND SLUGGING CROWN FOUR TIMES. MADE
2415 HITS. BATTED .300 OR OVER IN EACH
OF TEN YEARS WITH TOP OF .365 IN 1957.
TOPPED A.L. IN WALKS FIVE YEARS AND
IN RUNS SCORED SIX SEASONS. VOTED
MOST VALUABLE PLAYER 1956-57-62. NAMED
ON 20 A.L. ALL-STAR TEAMS. SET WORLD
SERIES RECORDS FOR HOMERS, 18; RUNS, 42;
RUNS BATTED IN, 40; TOTAL BASES, 123;
AND BASES ON BALLS, 43.

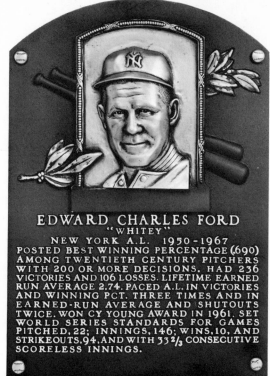

EDWARD CHARLES FORD
"WHITEY"
NEW YORK A.L. 1950-1967
POSTED BEST WINNING PERCENTAGE (.690)
AMONG TWENTIETH CENTURY PITCHERS
WITH 200 OR MORE DECISIONS. HAD 236
VICTORIES AND 106 LOSSES. LIFETIME EARNED
RUN AVERAGE 2.74. PACED A.L. IN VICTORIES
AND WINNING PCT. THREE TIMES AND IN
EARNED-RUN AVERAGE AND SHUTOUTS
TWICE. WON CY YOUNG AWARD IN 1961. SET
WORLD SERIES STANDARDS FOR GAMES
PITCHED, 22; INNINGS, 146; WINS, 10, AND
STRIKEOUTS, 94, AND WITH 33 2/3 CONSECUTIVE
SCORELESS INNINGS.

The 1961 New York Yankees. Front: Frank Prudenti, Fred Bengis (batboys). Front row (left to right): Whitey Ford, Bill Skowron, Hal Reniff, Jim Hegan, Frankie Crosetti, Ralph Houk, Johnny James, Wally Moses, Earl Torgeson, Clete Boyer, Yogi Berra, Mickey Mantle. Middle row: Billy Gardner, Bob Hale, Joe DeMaestri, Tony Kubek, Tex Clevenger, Ralph Terry, Hector Lopez, Bob Cerv, Elston Howard, Roger Maris, Bob Turley, Joe Soares (trainer). Back row: Bobby Richardson, Al Downing, Tom Tresh, Luis Arroyo, Johnny Blanchard, Bill Stafford, Roland Sheldon, Jim Coates, Spud Murray (batting practice pitcher), Buddy Daley, Bruce Henry (traveling secretary).

6

★★★★★★★

The M & M Boys
and the KC Connection

The 1961 New York Yankees

The New York Yankees held a stranglehold on the national sport from 1936 to 1964. During that time, they romped to 22 pennants and 16 World Series wins. A number of those teams could claim membership among baseball's eight best, but the one that stands out is the 1961 squad. Yankee bats thundered throughout the summer that year, belting a record 240 home runs. Their power show was so awesome that it may have intimidated American League hitters. Batters started overswinging, trying for home runs, and it was nine years before any American Leaguer topped the .330 mark. In eight of those years, it took at least 44 home runs to lead the league. But despite the new free-swinging style, no one could match the fireworks of the '61 Yanks.

Like most great teams, the Yankees had tremendous players in their peak years, a good supporting group, some pleasant surprises, and help from an unwitting foe. Mickey Mantle and Whitey Ford were the New York stars, and they both looked forward to good seasons in 1961. A long history of injuries had cut down on Mantle's playing time and left him in pain whenever he took the field. Yet he still showed speed in playing center field as well as a fine throwing arm and the skill to hit for both high average and home runs from either side of the plate. If he could avoid further injury, Mantle seemed a good bet to repeat his Most Valuable Player years of 1956 and 1957.

Ford, meanwhile, was finally going to get a chance to pitch every fourth day. Although he had been the Yanks' top hurler for years, the 5-foot, 10-inch lefty had never won 20 games. Under manager Casey Stengel, Ford had never been

53

Lovable Casey Stengel won more World Series games than any other manager in baseball. Yet the "Old Professor" was fired after a heart-breaking World Series loss to the Pirates in 1960.

allowed to start in more than 33 games a season. Stengel was gone now, and new manager Ralph Houk wanted Whitey on the mound as often as possible. Houk could hardly be blamed, because Ford owned a wicked curve ball and had one of the best winning percentages in the game.

It hardly seems fair to put Lawrence Peter Berra in with the supporting cast. But this Hall of Fame catcher, nicknamed Yogi from childhood, was winding down a long career. Once thought too clumsy to be a pro, he had become a top catcher and home-run hitter. Since Yogi's legs weren't what they used to be, New York had moved him to the outfield, where he remained a dangerous clutch hitter.

Moose Skowron, the veteran first baseman, added muscle to the lineup with 26 home runs in 1960. Elston Howard and Johnny Blanchard, the two catchers taking over for Berra, also looked as though they had home runs in their swings. As for defense, the Yanks were strongest where it was most important: up the middle. Tony Kubek, who had the skill to play any position, was installed as the shortstop. He teamed well with quick little Bobby Richardson

LAWRENCE PETER BERRA
"YOGI"
NEW YORK, A.L. 1946-1963
NEW YORK, N.L. 1965
PLAYED ON MORE PENNANT-WINNERS (14) AND
WORLD CHAMPIONS (10) THAN ANY PLAYER IN
HISTORY. HAD 358 HOME RUNS AND LIFETIME
.285 BATTING AVERAGE. SET MANY RECORDS
FOR CATCHERS, INCLUDING 148 CONSECUTIVE
GAMES WITHOUT AN ERROR. VOTED A. L. MOST
VALUABLE PLAYER 1951-54-55. MANAGED
YANKEES TO PENNANT IN 1964.

as the second baseman. People still had trouble believing the light-hitting Richardson had set a World Series record with 12 RBIs in 1960.

The Yankees were the last team that needed luck, yet they received a pleasant surprise in pitcher Luis Arroyo. A screwball artist who had shuffled around the National League for years without finding steady work, Arroyo had joined New York in 1959. Suddenly, he pulled himself together for a brief stint as the league's top reliever.

The author of such strange sayings as, "The game is never over until it's over," Yogi Berra won the American League's Most Valuable Player Award three times. None of the other legendary Yankee stars—Ruth, Gehrig, DiMaggio, or Mantle—could top that.

When discussing the '61 Yankees, there is no way to ignore the helpfulness of the Kansas City A's. When the Philadelphia A's relocated in Kansas City in 1953, the team's new owners had hired a man from the Yankee organization as their general manager. The A's and the Yankees got along so well that there seemed to be a shuttle bus running between them. Between 1953 and 1960, the teams completed 17 trades involving 68 players. At one time, nine members of the '61 Yankees had come from Kansas City. Two facts give an idea of who got the better of those deals. The '61 Yanks rank as one of baseball's all-time best; the '61 A's belong with the worst!

In 1957 the A's had sent third baseman Cletis Boyer to the Yankees. Although not a great hitter, the great Brooks Robinson called Boyer the best fielding third baseman he had seen. Two years later, pitcher Ralph Terry returned to New York after a couple of years in Kansas City. With new experience and confidence, he was ready to help out in the pennant race.

But the A's best gift of all was right fielder Roger Maris, who had also come in a 1959 trade. A left-handed pull hitter,

Pitcher Ralph Terry hit rock bottom when he served up the home run the cost the Yankees the 1960 World Series. He bounced back, however, to post a 16-3 mark in 1961.

Maris had an ideal swing for Yankee Stadium's short right field. Roger wasted no time proving his worth and won the 1960 American League Most Valuable Player Award with 39 homers and 112 RBIs.

From the start of the 1961 season, it was obvious that the Yankees were content to turn every game into a slugging match. Bunts and stolen bases were considered a waste of time. Five of the Yankee regulars totaled four stolen bases between them! The Yankees were aiming for the fences.

Maris needed 10 games to warm up before he blasted his first home run. But once he started, he sparked a home-run contest as exciting as the famous Ruth-Gehrig duel of 1927. Mantle and Maris, known as the M & M boys, traded home runs throughout the summer. Batting behind Maris in the lineup, Mantle was at a disadvantage. No one wanted to walk Maris with a slugger like Mantle coming up, so Roger saw plenty of good pitches to hit. On the other hand, Mantle received 126 walks during the year.

While the Yanks were tearing up league pitching, they still could not shake off a determined Detroit Tiger team. Led by hot-hitting Norm Cash and Al Kaline, the Tigers stayed in the pennant race until they faded in September. At the same time, Maris finally pulled away from Mantle and set off alone after Ruth's season record of 60 home runs. Hounded so badly by the press that his hair fell out in clumps, the nearly exhausted Maris finally caught up to Ruth and then passed him in the last week

Babe Ruth's record of 60 home runs in a season was such a legend that many resented Roger Maris for this 61st round trip in 1961.

of the season. Mantle, bothered again by injuries, finished with 54 to Maris' 61. That made the M & M boys the top home-run pair in history.

Pitchers facing New York also found the rest of the lineup loaded with danger. Moose Skowron pounded 28 homers, and Yogi Berra chipped in with 22.

Hall of Fame pitcher Whitey Ford won 20 games in a season only twice in his career, but there were only two seasons in which he lost more than 9 games. Here he handcuffs the Reds with a two-hit shutout in the 1961 World Series.

Elston Howard hit 21 to go with his .348 batting average. Despite playing less than half time, even reserve Johnny Blanchard collected 21 round trips.

Pitcher Whitey Ford found that his increased work load didn't bother him a bit. The curveball specialist won 25 while losing only 4. Right-hander Ralph Terry won 16 and lost 3, giving New York an overwhelming right-left duo. Although the rest of the staff was not outstanding, Luis Arroyo bailed them out of

trouble. He finished with a 15-5 mark, 29 saves, and a 2.19 ERA. As usual, the great hitting and pitching hid the fact that New York also owned the best fielding mark in the league.

World Series time was another chance for the Yanks to shine. Although they did not come close to their power show of the 1960 Series when they had scored 55 runs, they still won easily. Maris finished his season in a grand way, with a ninth-inning home run to win game three. Ford broke Babe Ruth's record of 28-2/3 scoreless World Series innings with his third-straight Fall Classic shutout. He was working on a fourth when a foot injury forced him to leave in the fifth inning of a game.

Few people, though, remember much about Ford's brilliant season. Instead the 1961 Yankees will always be remembered as the team that hit an incredible 240 home runs, a mark which has never been equalled.

Maris lashes a pitch from Boston's Tracy Stallard over the fence for home run number 61. "All it brought was headaches," Maris later said of his historic blast.

First baseman Moose Skowron (14) can't stretch far enough to make the play on Cincinnati's Gordy Coleman in the '61 Series. Skowron had better luck at the plate, however, and hit .353 with a home run and five RBIs.

THE 1961 NEW YORK YANKEES

Dynasty Years: 1949-1964

World Series Record:

1949 won over Brooklyn Dodgers, 4 games to 1
1950 won over Philadelphia Phillies, 4 games to 0
1951 won over New York Giants, 4 games to 2
1952 won over Brooklyn Dodgers, 4 games to 3
1953 won over Brooklyn Dodgers, 4 games to 2
1954 not in World Series
1955 lost to Brooklyn Dodgers, 4 games to 3
1956 won over Brooklyn Dodgers, 4 games to 3

1957 lost to Milwaukee Braves, 4 games to 3
1958 won over Milwaukee Braves, 4 games to 3
1959 not in World Series
1960 lost to Pittsburgh Pirates, 4 games to 3
1961 won over Cincinnati Reds, 4 games to 1
1962 won over San Francisco Giants, 4 games to 3
1963 lost to Los Angeles Dodgers, 4 games to 0
1964 lost to St. Louis Cardinals, 4 games to 3

1961 Record: 109-53 (8 games ahead of Detroit Tigers)

	R*	OR	BA	HR	SB	E	CG	ShO	ERA
New York	827	612	.263	**240**	28	**124**	47	14	3.46
Detroit·	**841**	671	.266	180	98	146	**62**	12	3.55
Baltimore	691	**588**	.254	149	39	128	54	**21**	**3.22**
Chicago	765	726	.265	138	**100**	128	39	3	4.06
Cleveland	737	752	.266	150	34	139	35	12	4.15
Boston	729	792	.254	112	56	144	35	6	4.29
Minnesota	707	778	.250	167	47	174	49	14	4.28
Los Angeles	744	784	.245	189	37	192	25	5	4.31
Kansas City	683	863	.247	90	58	175	32	5	4.74
Washington	618	776	.244	119	81	156	39	8	4.23

Top Hitters:			**Power Hitters:**		HR	RBI
	Elston Howard	.348		Roger Maris	61	142
	Mickey Mantle	.317		Mickey Mantle	54	128
	Johnny Blanchard	.305		Moose Skowron	28	89
	Tony Kubek	.276		Yogi Berra	22	61
				Elston Howard	21	77
				Johnny Blanchard	21	54

		Won	Lost	ERA	Saves
Starting Pitchers:	Whitey Ford	25	4	3.21	
	Ralph Terry	16	3	3.15	
	Bill Stafford	14	9	2.68	
	Rollie Sheldon	11	5	3.60	
Ace Relievers:	Luis Arroyo	15	5	2.19	29

* R=Runs, OR=Opponents' Runs, BA=Batting Average, HR=Home Runs, SB=Stolen Bases, E=Errors, CG=Complete Games by Starting Pitchers, ShO=Shutouts, ERA=Earned Run Average. **League leaders are shown in boldface type.**

Right: Manager Dick Williams' feisty personality dominated many of the teams he managed in his long career, but he more than met his match in trying to keep the turbulent A's in one piece in 1973.

Below: The 1973 Oakland A's. Front row (left to right): Reggie Jackson, Catfish Hunter, Pat Bourque, Ron Pieraldi (batboy), Dick Green, Vic Davalillo, Billy North. Second row: Bert Campaneris, Vida Blue, Paul Lindblad, Coach Jerry Adair, Coach Vern Hoscheit, Manager Dick Williams, Coach Irv Noren, Coach Wes Stock, Sal Bando, Gene Tenace. Third row: Joe Romo (trainer), Jim Bank (traveling secretary), Angel Mangual, Jesus Alou, Joe Rudi, Blue Moon Odom, Mike Andrews, Ted Kubiak, Frank Ciensczyk (equipment manager). Back row: Horacio Pina, Ken Holtzman, Deron Johnson, Rollie Fingers, Billy Conigliaro, Ray Fosse, Darold Knowles, Allan Lewis.

★★★7★★★

Even the A's Couldn't Beat the A's

The 1973 Oakland A's

The 1942 St. Louis Cardinals are fondly remembered as a perfect example of what teamwork can do. While not the most talented team, they played with such hustle and enthusiasm that they raced past National League teams to the pennant. Their extra effort and cooperation gave them a large edge over other more talented teams.

So how can the 1972-74 Oakland A's be explained? More A's were injured breaking up fights between teammates than were hurt on the field! The owner made it impossible for his manager to lead the team, and he made most of his players furious. Oakland pitchers stated openly that they were only playing for the money. The A's griped at everything, and they looked, spoke, and acted without any regard for team spirit. Although their seasonal records do not match others in this book, the A's must have

been an exceptional group to overcome their problems and win three straight World Series.

Oakland owner Charles Finley became known as one of baseball's all-time villains, but he did know how to collect great baseball players. With the smallest office staff in the game and no general manager, Finley still turned the hapless A's into contenders. Using some of the millions he had made in the insurance business, Finley turned his scouts loose, armed with open checkbooks. During 1964-65, he signed pitchers Jim Hunter, John Odom, and Rollie Fingers, and hitters Rick Monday, Reggie Jackson, Sal Bando, and Joe Rudi.

By 1968 these young players had brought the A's (who had moved to Oakland that year) their first winning season in the club's 15 years. After battling the next two years for their divisional title, they won it in 1971 with a 101-60 record. Continuing their determined climb, the A's went on to the World Series in 1972, where they edged Cincinnati, four games to three. Experts looked to the 1973 season to see if the A's were for real, or if they had just been lucky.

Oakland looked to its pitching staff to lead the way in defending their title. The top hurler was Jim Hunter, known as Catfish simply because owner Finley decided he needed a flashy title. As it turned out, Hunter did not need gimmicks to make a name for himself. A man with tremendous control of his pitches, Hunter was a baffling opponent. Most batters were convinced they could pound Catfish's "easy" pitches. But when they swung, the ball didn't go anywhere! After posting his second straight 21-win year in 1972, Hunter was in top form.

Finley wasn't as successful in pushing a nickname on pitcher Vida Blue, the most devastating lefty since Sandy Koufax. After Blue broke in with the A's in 1971, Finley tried to get him to change his first name to True. Out of that minor quarrel grew major grudges, and the

Oakland's pitching aces wasted no time in grabbing headlines. In his rookie season, Catfish Hunter (above) pitched a perfect game. Vida Blue (below)—later traded to the Giants—broke in with a 24-8 record, 8 shutouts, and 301 strikeouts.

bitter Blue lost his enthusiasm for the game. Still, Oakland fans hoped that Vida could bounce back to his 1971 form when he had won 24 games and struck out 301 batters.

Oakland's third starting hurler was Ken Holtzman, who had come from the Cubs in 1971 in exchange for Rick Monday. Like Blue, Holtzman was left-handed and suspicious of baseball owners. His 19-11 record and 2.51 ERA in 1972 gave Oakland three of the best starters in the game.

With such capable starters, there seemed little need for a bullpen crew. Yet Oakland's relievers were as good as the starters. Reliable Rollie Fingers, handlebar mustache and all, had pulled his team out of countless jams with his sinker. Just to be on the safe side, Finley had added veterans Darold Knowles, Horacio Pina, and Paul Lindblad to the staff before the 1973 season.

Oakland rarely hit for high average, but they made their hits count. Leading the charge was fast-talking right fielder Reggie Jackson. A hard swinger who struck out often, Reggie connected often enough to be one of the league's most feared long-ball hitters. While

Clean-shaven Rollie Fingers was a bust as a starter for the A's, notching only 7 wins in 21 decisions. Sporting a magnificent mustache, Fingers was almost unbeatable coming out of the bullpen.

Jackson considered himself to be one of the game's most complete players, left fielder Joe Rudi had a stronger claim to that honor. Always a smooth fielder, Rudi had gradually learned the art of batting. In 1972 he hit .305 with 19 home runs and a league-leading 9 triples.

The A's lineup included two infielders who sometimes lagged near the bottom of the league in average, but they had a knack of getting hits when it counted the most. Despite hitting only .236 in 1972, third baseman Sal Bando had driven in 77 runs. Gene Tenace had batted only .225 with 5 home runs during the regular season. But he burst into the headlines with 4 homers in the '72 World Series.

When speed was needed, the A's turned to Bert Campaneris and new center fielder Billy North. Campy could probably do more things well on the field than any man in the game. In the minors, he had once pitched right-handed to right-handed batters and left-handed to lefties! He had played all nine positions in one game in 1965. Now the six-time base-stealing champ had settled down to being just a fine short-stop. North had come over from the Cubs to fill Oakland's biggest weakness of 1972: center field. Finley also hired track star Herb Washington as a pinch runner.

The one thing Finley could not do was keep his players happy and working together. The A's griped and second-guessed the manager on his handling of pitchers. They said whatever was on their minds, called each other names, and scuffled in the locker room. Jackson, Fingers, Odom, and North were among players who ended up in fights. Owner Finley overruled his manager, Dick Williams, on decisions and got into shouting matches with his players, especially Jackson.

Despite all of this turmoil, the A's rode Catfish Hunter's great pitching to the top of their division in 1973. Hunter, working on a 15-3 record at the All-Star break, had his sights set on 30 wins. But he was hit on the thumb by a line drive in that All-Star game and was put out of action for nearly a month. He came back just in time to help the bickering A's beat out the Kansas City Royals by six games in the American League West.

With Hunter finishing at 21-5 and

In this game against the Mets in the 1973 World Series, Reggie Jackson built the foundation for his "Mr. October" reputation with two doubles and a single.

Holtzman and Blue muttering their way to 21-13 and 20-9, the A's were never in danger of falling into a losing streak. Blue Moon Odom's arm troubles, however, left Oakland short of a fourth starter and kept the bullpen hopping. Rollie Fingers saved 22 games with an ERA of 1.92, and Darold Knowles saved 9 more.

Oakland's unimpressive offense of 1972 was boosted by great 1973 seasons from the three power men: Jackson, Bando, and Tenace. Big Reggie won the Most Valuable Player Award on the strength of his 32 home runs, .293 aver-age, and league-leading 117 RBIs. With a career-high average of .285, Bando clouted 29 homers and knocked in 98 runs. Tenace, rewarded for his 1972 World Series with a starting job, chipped in with 24 home runs. When the big guys weren't blasting in runs, Campaneris and North were stealing them and combined for 87 stolen bases and 187 runs.

The 1973 World Series found the A's at their worst and best. Second baseman Mike Andrews made a couple of 12th inning errors to give the Mets game two of the Series. An outraged Finley pulled Andrews off the team, claiming the player was injured. Andrews' teammates responded by blasting Finley in the newspapers and spreading rumors of a strike for the rest of the Series.

After game four, it seemed that the A's had finally dug themselves into a hole too big to get out of. The Mets had taken a three-games-to-two lead and sent ace pitcher Tom Seaver to wrap up the championship. Unfortunately for Seaver, he was up against a great pressure pitcher, and Catfish evened the Series with a masterful 3-1 victory. Oakland then captured the title in game seven. The difference in the series was Oakland relievers Fingers and Knowles. Knowles appeared in all seven games without giving up an earned run, and Fingers allowed only one in his six games. No Oakland victory could be quite complete without some bitterness, though. Manager Williams announced that he had taken all he could stomach and would not be back next year.

Oakland went on to win the World Series again in 1974, becoming the first team in 20 years to win three straight titles. No other team has accomplished so much under such bizarre conditions.

No, it's not a rugby match, just those wild and crazy A's! Somewhere in that pile is pitcher Darold Knowles, who got the final out of the Series for the champs.

THE 1973 OAKLAND A'S

Dynasty Years: 1972-1974

Play-off Record:
1972 won over Detroit Tigers, 3 games to 2
1973 won over Baltimore Orioles, 3 games to 2
1974 won over Baltimore Orioles, 3 games to 1

World Series Record:
1972 won over Cincinnati Reds, 4 games to 3
1973 won over New York Mets, 4 games to 3
1974 won over Los Angeles Dodgers, 4 games to 1

1973 Record: 94-68 (6 games ahead of Kansas City Royals)

	R*	OR	BA	HR	SB	E	CG	ShO	ERA
Oakland	**758**	615	.260	147	128	137	46	16	3.29
Baltimore	754	**561**	.266	119	**146**	119	67	14	**3.08**
Boston	738	647	.267	147	114	127	67	10	3.65
Kansas City	755	752	.261	114	105	167	40	7	4.21
Detroit	642	674	.254	157	28	**112**	39	11	3.90
Minnesota	738	692	**.270**	120	87	139	48	**18**	3.77
New York	641	610	.261	131	45	156	47	16	3.33
California	629	657	.253	93	59	156	**72**	3	3.57
Chicago	652	705	.256	111	84	144	48	15	3.87
Milwaukee	708	731	.253	145	110	145	50	11	3.98
Cleveland	680	826	.256	**158**	60	139	55	9	4.58
Texas	619	844	.255	110	91	161	35	10	4.64

				HR	RBI
Top Hitters:	Reggie Jackson	.293	**Power Hitters:** Reggie Jackson	32	117
	Sal Bando	.287	Sal Bando	29	98
	Bill North	.285	Gene Tenace	24	84
	Joe Rudi	.270	Deron Johnson	19	81

		Won	Lost	ERA	Saves
Starting Pitchers:	Catfish Hunter	21	5	3.34	
	Ken Holtzman	21	13	2.97	
	Vida Blue	20	9	3.28	
	Blue Moon Odom	5	12	4.49	
Ace Relievers:	Rollie Fingers	7	8	1.92	22
	Darold Knowles	6	8	3.09	9
	Horacio Pina	6	3	2.76	8

* R=Runs, OR=Opponents' Runs, BA=Batting Average, HR=Home Runs, SB=Stolen Bases, E=Errors, CG=Complete Games by Starting Pitchers, ShO=Shutouts, ERA=Earned Run Average. **League leaders are shown in boldface type.**

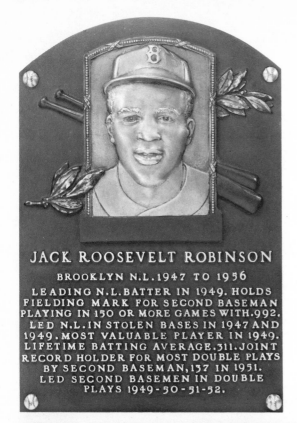

JACK ROOSEVELT ROBINSON

BROOKLYN N.L. 1947 TO 1956

LEADING N.L. BATTER IN 1949. HOLDS
FIELDING MARK FOR SECOND BASEMAN
PLAYING IN 150 OR MORE GAMES WITH .992.
LED N.L. IN STOLEN BASES IN 1947 AND
1949. MOST VALUABLE PLAYER IN 1949.
LIFETIME BATTING AVERAGE .311. JOINT
RECORD HOLDER FOR MOST DOUBLE PLAYS
BY SECOND BASEMAN, 137 IN 1951.
LED SECOND BASEMEN IN DOUBLE
PLAYS 1949-50-51-52.

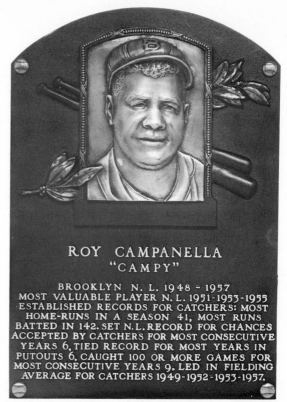

ROY CAMPANELLA
"CAMPY"

BROOKLYN N.L. 1948 - 1957
MOST VALUABLE PLAYER N.L. 1951-1953-1955
ESTABLISHED RECORDS FOR CATCHERS: MOST
HOME-RUNS IN A SEASON 41, MOST RUNS
BATTED IN 142. SET N.L. RECORD FOR CHANCES
ACCEPTED BY CATCHERS FOR MOST CONSECUTIVE
YEARS 6, TIED RECORD FOR MOST YEARS IN
PUTOUTS 6, CAUGHT 100 OR MORE GAMES FOR
MOST CONSECUTIVE YEARS 9. LED IN FIELDING
AVERAGE FOR CATCHERS 1949-1952-1953-1957.

The 1955 Brooklyn Dodgers. Front: Charlie DiGiovanna (batboy). Front row (left to right): George Shuba, Don Zimmer, Coach Joe Becker, Coach Jake Pitler, Manager Walter Alston, Coach Billy Herman, Pee Wee Reese, Dixie Howell, Sandy Amoros, Roy Campanella. Middle row: John Griffen (clubhouse man), Carl Erskine, Sandy Koufax, Lee Scott (in dark suit), Roger Craig, Don Newcombe, Karl Spooner, Don Hoak, Carl Furillo, Frank Kellert, Doc Wendler. Back row: Russ Meyer, Jim Gilliam, Billy Loes, Clem Labine, Gil Hodges, Ed Roebuck, Don Bessent, Duke Snider, Johnny Podres, Rube Walker, Jackie Robinson.

★★★ 8 ★★★
Any Club Could Have Done It

The 1955 Brooklyn Dodgers

Any club in pro baseball could have built a championship team in the 1940s. It wouldn't have taken much money or luck or the shrewd sense to hoodwink another team into a bad trade. All that was needed was some courage and foresight.

The Brooklyn Dodgers happened to be run by a man with plenty of both. General manager Branch Rickey saw the growing pool of talented players forming in the Negro leagues. He knew that only an unwritten rule barring blacks from the major leagues kept these men from becoming stars. Secretly, Rickey developed a plan for opening the league's doors to blacks. In so doing, he rounded up the cream of players from the Negro leagues before his opponents could join the bandwagon.

Brooklyn's black pioneers, together with Rickey's carefully organized farm system, launched a decade of greatness for the Dodgers. The Dodgers just missed notching some of the top records of all time. Had Brooklyn won just 4 more of the nearly 1,700 games they played between 1946 and 1956, they would have captured 9 pennants in 11 years! What has hurt the club most in ratings of the best all-time teams was their failure to win big games. Brooklyn lost its first seven World Series appearances. Such mysterious streaks become harder to break the longer they go on. Because of this, we'll give the credit to the Dodger team that finally broke the championship jinx in 1955.

Branch Rickey knew what kind of abuse the league's first black player would have to face. After careful consideration, he chose an all-around athlete named Jackie Robinson to break the color barrier. With his daring base-

As he signs a contract with the Dodgers on April 10, 1947, Jackie Robinson's pen wipes out baseball's color barrier.

running, hitting, and fielding, Robinson brought a special excitement to the game that Rickey felt all fans could appreciate. But despite Robinson's talent, his rookie season of 1947 was a ticklish time. Jackie heard the insults and threats that teams would refuse to play the Dodgers. He was determined, though, to keep his mind on his job.

When the year ended, Robinson was voted Rookie of the Year. Two years later, he shamed critics who thought blacks couldn't compete by batting .342 with 16 home runs and 37 stolen bases to win the National League Most Valuable Player Award.

When other teams started scrambling to find good black players, they found that the Dodgers already had many of the best under contract. Three of the Dodgers' new stars won Rookie of the Year honors between 1949 and 1953: pitchers Don Newcombe and Joe Black and all-purpose man Junior Gilliam.

But the one who did not get the award may have been the best of them all. Big Roy Campanella broke in with the Dodgers as a catcher in 1948. Campy was an inspiring player who truly seemed to love the game of baseball. A powerful right-handed hitter, he won Most Valuable Player awards in three different years.

Those players could have made any team a serious contender. When added to the products of the Dodgers' minor league system, it spelled trouble for the National League. Without giving away huge bonuses, the tight-fisted Rickey built a lineup designed to take advantage of the short Ebbetts Field fences. Campanella was joined by Gil Hodges, Duke Snider, and Carl Furillo to form a dangerous offensive punch. Hodges had switched from the outfield to first base early in his career. Hard work had made him a fine fielder as well as an explosive hitter. With his blend of speed, high

Roy Campanella said a person had to have a little kid in him to play pro baseball. There was enough of a kid in Campy to earn three National League Most Valuable Player awards.

Had they been able to solve the Yankee hex, the Dodgers would have boasted baseball's most famous lineup in the 1950s. Key performers among them were (left to right) Junior Gilliam, Pee Wee Reese, Duke Snider, and Jackie Robinson.

average, and power, Snider rivaled the other great center fielders of his day, Willie Mays and Mickey Mantle. Furillo, who had led the league in hitting in 1953 with a .344 average, contributed a line-drive batting stroke.

Perhaps the key Dodger, though, was the one player who had been with Brooklyn since before Rickey had come.

Shortstop Pee Wee Reese held the club together with shortstop play and his experienced leadership. Veteran sports-writer Fred Lieb listed Reese, Robinson, Hodges, and Campanella as baseball's best at their positions from 1950 to 1975.

Despite all of these stars, however, the Dodgers could not break the Yan-kees' hex in the World Series. After yet

The saying, "Those who can't do, teach," certainly applied to Dodger manager Walt Alston. Although he struck out in his only time at bat in the major leagues, Alston guided the Dodgers to 2,040 wins and seven pennants.

another failure with their strong 1953 team, the Dodgers had to be discouraged. Under new manager Walt Alston in 1954, they barely challenged the New York Giants. The rival Giants made it all the more bitter by winning *their* World Series in four straight.

There was no reason to think that 1955 would be Brooklyn's year. Campanella and Newcombe were big question marks. Bothered by a hand injury, Campy had slumped to .207 in 1954. And after two years in military service, Newcombe had been so rusty that he won only nine games. The rest of the pitching staff did not have the look of a champion. Veteran Carl Erskine was starting to slow down, and fastball thrower Johnny Podres couldn't stay healthy. Breakingball pitcher Billy Loes hadn't come through the way scouts had expected. That forced the Dodgers to rely heavily on relievers Clem Labine and Ed Roebuck.

Despite these problems, the Dodgers quickly sprinted into the lead. Everything seemed to be going right, and they won their first 10 games and 21 of their first 23. In a state of shock, the National League began to realize the

Edwin "Duke" Snider blasted a total of 11 home runs in six World Series against the Yankees. Until 1955, his efforts were largely wasted.

pennant race was over before it had even started. With their heavy hitters taking aim at the fences, Brooklyn raced to a 55-22 record midway through the year, 13-1/2 games ahead of the field. Keeping the pressure on, the Dodgers won the pennant on September 8, the earliest it had ever been clinched in the National League.

Duke Snider led the way with 42 home runs and a .309 average. Not far behind was a recharged Campanella with 32 homers and a .318 mark. Furillo added a .314 mark and 26 homers, while Hodges "slumped" to .289 and 27. Reese plugged the shortstop hole as well as ever, and only Robinson began to show signs of slowing down.

Big Don Newcombe got back into the swing of things with a 20-5 mark. Even though they had no other dependable starters, Brooklyn still led the National League in ERA as well as runs. Labine and Roebuck took turns sharing 23 saves.

Impressive as the Dodgers had been, no one could take them too seriously in the World Series. Their old tormentors, the Yankees, were back again. It was just like old times as New York took the first two games of the Series.

"Now we're getting somewhere!" the Dodger batboy seems to be saying after Gil Hodges' home run triggered a Brooklyn rally in game four of the 1955 Series.

With Dodger ace Don Newcombe hopelessly caught in the Yankee jinx, Brooklyn was forced to rely on young Johnny Podres to pitch game seven.

No team had ever come back to win the championship after losing the first two games. Suddenly, though, the Dodger bats let loose years of frustration. Snider tore into Yankee pitching for four home runs, and Campanella added two. Searching for a pitcher who could stop the Yankees, the Dodgers finally settled on Johnny Podres.

Coming off a dismal 9-10 record that season, Podres found his fastball in the World Series. After winning game three, Podres came back to pitch the seventh and deciding game. Helped by a brilliant running catch by left fielder Sandy Amoros, Podres shut down the Yanks. The Dodgers' tense 2-0 victory had finally earned them a championship!

With that final hurdle cleared at last, the Dodgers began to do well in title games. After losing in 1956, they won their next three World Series in 1959, 1963, and 1965. The running start given them by their black players carried them a long, long way.

THE 1955 BROOKLYN DODGERS

Dynasty Years: 1952-1956

World Series Record:

1952 lost to New York Yankees, 4 games to 3
1953 lost to New York Yankees, 4 games to 2
1954 not in World Series

1955 won over New York Yankees, 4 games to 3
1956 lost to New York Yankees, 4 games to 3

1955 Record: 98-55 (13.5 games ahead of Milwaukee Braves)

	R*	OR	BA	HR	SB	E	CG	ShO	ERA
Brooklyn	**857**	**650**	**.271**	**201**	**79**	133	46	11	**3.68**
Milwaukee	743	668	.261	182	42	152	**61**	5	3.85
New York	702	673	.260	169	38	142	52	6	3.77
Philadelphia	675	666	.255	132	44	**110**	58	11	3.93
Cincinnati	761	684	.270	181	51	139	38	**12**	3.95
Chicago	626	713	.247	164	37	147	47	10	4.17
St. Louis	654	757	.261	143	64	146	42	10	4.56
Pittsburgh	560	767	.244	91	22	166	41	5	4.39

Top Hitters:			**Power Hitters:**		HR	RBI
	Roy Campanella	.318		Duke Snider	42	136
	Carl Furillo	.314		Roy Campanella	32	107
	Duke Snider	.309		Gil Hodges	27	102
	Gil Hodges	.289		Carl Furillo	26	95
	Pee Wee Reese	.282				

		Won	Lost	ERA	Saves
Starting Pitchers:	Don Newcombe	20	5	3.20	
	Carl Erskine	11	8	3.79	
	Billy Loes	10	4	3.59	
	Johnny Podres	9	10	3.95	
Ace Relievers:	Clem Labine	13	5	3.24	11
	Ed Roebuck	5	6	4.71	12
	Don Bessent	8	1	2.70	3

* R=Runs, OR=Opponents' Runs, BA=Batting Average, HR=Home Runs, SB=Stolen Bases, E=Errors, CG=Complete Games by Starting Pitchers, ShO=Shutouts, ERA=Earned Run Average. **League leaders are shown in boldface type.**

ACKNOWLEDGMENTS: The photographs are reproduced through the courtesy of: pp. 1, 8, 9, 10, 13, 14, 15, 16, 18, 20, 21, 22, 23, 24, 28 (bottom), 31, 36, 38, 39, 40, 44, 46, 47, 52, 54, 55, 56, 59, 60, 62, 64 (top), 70, 73, 74, 76, 77, National Baseball Hall of Fame and Museum, Inc.; pp. 2, 34, 57, 58, 67, 68, 72, 78, 80, AP/Wide World Photos; p. 26, Chicago Historical Society; pp. 28 (top), 30, 32, Cincinnati Reds, Inc.; p. 41, Baltimore Orioles; pp. 49, 50, 65, UPI/Bettmann Archive; p. 64 (bottom), San Francisco Giants; p. 75, Los Angeles Dodgers, Inc.

The Reds couldn't get a baseball passed Brooks Robinson either in the field or at the plate in the 1971 World Series, proving here to batter Johnny Bench that good defense beats good offense. Robinson led the Orioles' demonstration of why they may have been the best glove men in baseball history.